I HEARD THE TULUGAK SQUAWK

Tracilyn George

©2016 Tracilyn George

Contents

PROLOGUE 4
HOUSE PARTY AT THE TREE HOUSE 6
A NIGHT AT THE BIG BAR 10
ARMED ESCORT 15
AND I DON'T LIKE YOU EITHER 21
GIMME ALL YOU'RE MONEY! 25
ALL HE HAD TO DO WAS ASK 30
IF ONLY I HAD BEEN WITH HER 36
WHERE ARE YOUR EYES? 40
WOULDN'T IT BE FUNNY IF-? 45
MIDGE 48
TRACILYN, IS IT FUNNY? 51
HALBERT 54
HOW WAS I SUPPOSED TO KNOW? 56
MOMENTARY MELTDOWN 60
WHAT HAPPENED TO SUNDAY? 63
YOUR TEAM IS GOING DOWN TOMORROW! 66
FORTY LASHINGS WITH A WET NOODLE 70
SECURITY! 73
EPILOGUE 76

PROLOGUE

Many people cringe at the thought of going to the Arctic for a multitude of reasons. The main one is because of the extreme temperature. I'm not going to lie and say it doesn't get cold in winter because the numbers can dip to -50° or -60° Celsius.

But, unlike many places in other parts of the country, there is no huge fluctuation in numbers. Once it hits the below zero, it stays there for weeks. There is never -40 one day then +2 the next. You become quickly acclimatized to it. Plus, if you dress properly, the weather will not be an issue.

You will also not miss out on the spectacular wonders of the north. You'll see a variety of wildlife and the Aurora Borealis – a brilliant light show put on for free every night. Pictures and words do not do it justice. You need to immerse yourself in it – feel it, see it, and play with it.

My time in the Canadian Arctic has had a profound effect on my life. There were both negative and positive experiences which happened to me – changing my views on the world and life in general. The negative showed me I was stronger than I thought and the positive enriched my softer side.

The Arctic and I have a love-hate relationship. I love it when I'm away from it, missing its unique and quirky personality. It seems to call out to me, beckoning me to come back as if it misses me too. Yet, when I am there, it finds different ways to make me want to leave and never want to come back.

The breakup is always messy – each one seemingly worse than the one before it. I am always bitter when I leave as it is with most turbulent endings of unhealthy relationships. But, once I've settled down and take a good look back, I realized things were not quite as bad as my imagination made it out to be. Yes, there were some major events that made me question why I went but the good experiences far outnumbered the bad.

The following stories are true stories – things that happened to me while I was living and working in the Arctic. Many names have been changed, partly because I do not remember them and partly to protect the identities of some.

HOUSE PARTY AT THE TREE HOUSE

In Norman Wells, you are limited in the activities in which you can participate. There is curling, hockey and drinking, the latter being the most common. Norman Wells has two bars, affectionately nicknamed Big Bar and Little Bar as well as a Legion and a liquor agency. Most people have house parties, get-togethers where many of the guests have a tendency to drink to excess.

The majority of those who live and work in the north come from away. I was from Nova Scotia; my roommate was from Ontario. We both worked for a small airline based out of Norman Wells. I was the dispatcher and she was one of the small crew of pilots.

One night, my roommate, Anne, was waiting for one of the guys to pick her up for a house party. I was more than content to stay home and watch a move but Derek, one of the mechanics, had other ideas.

"C'mon, Nova Scotia girl," he quipped. "We can't have you sitting home watching the weather station when there's a party to go to. You know we have a reputation to keep up."

How could I argue with that? Bluenosers and Newfoundlanders are regarded among the Canadian population of being "party" people. For the most part, we're easy-going, and laid back; we enjoy a good time whenever and wherever possible.

I find we enjoy laughing, dancing and lots of music of all kinds. So, up I went to my first northern house party. When we arrived, I was in awe of the house. It was log cabin style and two of the young pilots were renting it. They affectionately called their home the tree house, for obvious reasons. Jacob gave me the tour of the two-storey house before I started socializing with the others.

After getting a bottle of beer, I settled in the living room for an hour or so, talking with some of my co-workers. My second stop was the kitchen and dining room area, once I picked up a second beer. There were fewer people but a lot brighter so it took me a bit to adjust to the light.

I took a seat across from Luke, one of the senior pilots. His wife, Lori, sat next to him. It was nice to spend time with my fellow workers and talk about anything but work. I was nearly done my third bottle when Jake asked me if I wanted a stronger drink than beer. At first, I declined. I knew what mixing alcohol did to me and the last thing I wanted was to get sloshed at my first get-together with my colleagues.

Just a quick background on me and drinking. I am not a mean or bad drunk but I do get quite chatty and silly. For the most part, I remember what I've done and how I've gotten from point A to point B. But, I have had my moments of blurred memory. At this stage of my life, it really is no big deal as there are more important things for me to worry about than how I got home from a night of binge drinking.

Once I finished my beer (three in about three hours); I decided to take Jake up on his offer of a harder drink but I would have to create my own concoction. My drink was comprised of Captain Morgan Dark Rum, Bailey's Irish Cream and Southern Comfort.

Jake had turned his nose up at it but once I had him try it, he loved it. In fact, he enjoyed it so much he took my large glass around to everyone so they could have a taste. By the time he returned to the kitchen, the glass was empty and I had to prepare a refill for myself.

Around midnight, my roommate had decided she was heading home but I decided to stick around for a little while longer. Couple more glasses of my invention – drunk very quickly – had loosened me up somewhat and was beginning to relax. Plus, I was enjoying my drink so much; I was guzzling them back like water.

Big mistake! By the time everyone was ready to leave, I was wasted. I remember standing between the bathroom and the front door, almost in trance. The next thing I knew, a pair of hands grabbed me by the shoulders and threw me into the bathroom.

"Don't come out until you're done!" a voice stated. To this day, I don't know who it was but the only thing I can do now is laugh about it. Let's just say, I don't drink like that any longer. Actually, I rarely even drink and I wonder how I could have been so stupid in the first place.

When I finished emptying my stomach, Jake put on my coat and placed me outside in the fresh, cold air.

"I called a cab forya. Do you have enough to get home?"he asked.

I nodded very slowly so not to disturb my now settled abdomen. Thankfully, I had the next day off so I could sleep off my hangover.

A NIGHT AT THE BIG BAR

A few weeks after the house party, my employer – North-Wright Airways – hosted Christmas reception at their office and hangar. Representatives of the various businesses around town were invited along with the staff of the company. As I was still in recovery mode from my binge a few short weeks before, I avoided the alcohol all together and opted for Diet Coke. With Diet Coke, the only after-effect would be the caffeine high followed by the lethargic aftermath.

With glass in hand, I made a bee-line to the hangar where some of my co-workers and guests were mingling. I found a space against the wall so I could watch the goings-on around me. One of the traits I have is being a people watcher. I absolutely love observing people in all situations and taking note of their reactions. In this case, there were lots of different personalities together in a social situation which meant anything could happen. If it did, it should be quite interesting.

But as much as I tried to blend into the background, being left to myself to observe my surroundings was not going to happen. One of North-Wrights agents, Elmo, approached me and started talking to me.

Considering he was beyond drunk, I had no clue as to what he was trying to tell me. I tried to act as if I understood to the best of my ability and I doubt that Elmo even realized he wasn't making any sense. It felt as if I was trapped and I had no escape.

Luckily for me, one of the pilots came over and interrupted. "Traci, come help me pick out some songs," announced Keith.

I quickly responded, "Okay, let's go."

After we were at the CD player, Keith said, "It looked like you needed to be rescued."

I nodded. "Thank you. I had no way of getting away from him and I had no idea what he was saying." Keith – my hero; I will be forever grateful to you, my friend.

After the party was over, a group of us headed to the Big Bar. A stand-up comic was flown in from down south to perform. Now, down south to those of us living in Norman Wells usually meantgoing to Edmonton. Not exactly a tropical paradise but more so than the Wells. It was a treat for us to have some live entertainment.

I have long forgotten his name but I found him quite amusing. It usually doesn't take much to make me laugh. You have to be really horrible for me not to laugh. There is a saying among my friends that if I don't laugh, it means you aren't funny.

Keith asked me what I wanted to drink. "What the hell is Moosehead?" he asked when I told him.

My brow knitted. "Nova Scotia beer but I'll take a Keith's."Unlike at the tree house, I vowed I was not going to drink to excess and I was going to limit myself to the type of beverage I was going to have.

After the comedian completed his last set, the DJ came on. The dance floor was afair size compared to other bars I had frequented. Keith and I were chatting about nothing when Terry, from Enbridge, approached us. It was obvious, at least tome, Terry had had a few drinks too many. He had that goofy, droopy-eyed glazed look upon his face.

Terry wasn't very tall – maybe about5'4" or so. Considering I'm only about five feet, his line of sight is not that far from my chest and I'm used to guys looking at my chest. It bothers some women to have men ogle them but it doesn't bother me at all. I'm also used to various comments about my large breasts and I reiterate, it doesn't bother me in the least.

So when Terry stared at my chest and said, "God, you have beautiful breasts," I wasn't the least bit phased by it. I actually found it quite funny because he had stated it so matter-of-factly in a drunken slur.

But Keith took offense. He, too, had quite a bit to drink. Keith grabbed Terry bythe front of his shirt. "Look, buddy," he shouted. "You can't talk to her like that. She's North-Wright property and she deserves respect."

Terry just stared back in a drunken stupor, oblivious to what was going on around him. I found it extremely humorous to watch these two drunken men at each other. Well, one at the other and the other completely clueless.

At work the following Monday, I mentioned the incident to Keith. "I'm pretty sure I could have handled him," I said.

Keith laughed. "In our condition, you probably could've taken us both on."

ARMED ESCORT

About four months into my stint in Norman Wells, I was beginning to feel restless. I think I may have been a gypsy in previous life because I find it very difficult to settle in one place for any length of time. Other than my hometown, I've never been in another place for more than one year. Even my work situations tend to change frequently. I get bored very easily so I need a change of venue to keep me from losing my mind.

So like I said, four months in and I needed to get out. I loved the town and the people I worked with but hated the job. To this day, I feel I was not properly trained and may have stayed on longer but for that reason alone.

Even my roommate at the time thought was improperly trained for the job. She believed the person I was replace had wanted to be asked to stay so she purposely tried to sabotage my job.

At this point, it really didn't matter. I was unhappy and needed to leave. I don't believe in staying somewhere and doing something if you are not happy. So I gave my notice and begrudgingly reported to work each day until they found areplacement.

At the end of my work term, I thought I had things wrapped up including a place to stay until my flight left in the middle of February. Turned out, I was wrong about my accommodations.

When I showed up at Eric's home, I was informed I couldn't stay because he had a friend from out of town visiting. He did compromise in allowing my luggage to stay and for me to shower there.

Where was I going to stay, you ask? Easy – in the community church that was near Eric's home. Fact is, Eric's house was once the manse. So off I go to the church and try to sleep on one of the pews. I don't remember getting much, if any.

The next morning, I shuffled over to the house for a shower. The place was in shambles. "What's going on?" I asked.

Eric wasn't certain how he should answer, or even if he should. "Jesse freaked out last night," he finally said. "He was mad because you were here."

I knitted my brow. "But I wasn't here. I was sleeping in the church, in case you had forgotten," I responded, upset.

Eric sighed. "I know but he still feels you're invading our weekend."

What could I say? I understood the misconception. My whole life is a study in misconceptions. "I'm sorry he feels that way. This wasn't the plan."

Eric decided not to pursue the issue any further. I think he knew it wouldn't do him any good to try. He did give me a bed to sleep on that night. Actually, he offered me the sofa which would be much more comfortable than church pew and I gladly accepted. As I didn't get much sleep, I opted to skip the service the next morning and catch up.

Before that could happen, I was informed – again – that I had to leave. For whatever reason, Eric just couldn't make up his mind and he didn't seem to have much of a backbone.

He did promise to find me a place to stay but at this point, I wasn't holding my breath. He had broken so many promises up to this point; I just couldn't find it in my heart to trust him.

After church, I was told that I offered the sofa of John and Tess. I was relieved since I truly liked the couple. John was out of town but Tess was certain he wouldn't mind me as a houseguest. I was even willing to-do odd jobs around the building they maintained to earn my keep.

Knowing that I hadn't slept in two days with all the commotion, Tess brought me out a pillow and blanket so I could sleep on the sofa. Needless to say, I crashed almost before my head hit the pillow. I don't remember waking up but I remember hearing voices.

The voices belonged to John and Tess and they were discussing my situation. "She is one of Jesus' lambs," said John. "She is lost but He is looking out for her." I smiled to myself. These people were truly of God and I appreciate them to this day.

When I fully woke up, I went to take a shower. John and Tess were out and I thought this would be a good time to call home. I had searched my luggage and my plane ticket to Halifax was gone. I called my father collect and explained to him the situation. He said he would get back to me.

About an hour or so later, Tess had returned and we were talking in the kitchen while having a cup of coffee. A knock on the door startled the two of us.

We were surprised to see the RCMP standing on the opposite side.

"Is Tracilyn here?" asked one of them. When I nodded, he waved me outside to talk in private.

"Your father contacted the RCMP detachment in Cole Harbour. Apparently, a friend of the family is a Mountie there. You know you could have come to our detachment here.

We would have been able to help you out. Sleeping in a church is not a good plan. You know that, right?" he asked. I answered yes.

He smiled. "We're going to get you home. We were told of your situation and we have ways of sending you home. Just don't let me hear of you sleeping in a church anymore." They were very sweet. I always had a thing for cops and this only added tomy fetish.

They grabbed my luggage and led met the Jimmy. There's nothing like alarmed escort to the airport and to the airline counter. I felt like a movie star.

After I had been home for a while, I was doing a contract job at Stats Canada. On my break, I was talking to one of the ladies I was working with and I told her I just returned from Norman Wells.

She asked me if I knew Norm. I said that I did, he was the RCMP officer who helped me come home. She told me he was her nephew. I quickly learned how small this world really is.

AND I DON'T LIKE YOU EITHER

In Iqaluit, anger and resentment runs rampant and deep within the hearts of some of the Inuit. In their brief history with white people, they have been enslaved, beaten and / or killed. Not all of the Inuit I had encountered in Iqaluit hated Caucasians but many did. Most of the time, the resentment surfaced after they had been drinking.

I understand their bitterness. No group of people should be subjected to hatred because of the color of their skin, what they believe in or where they originated. Genocide has been a part of our world's history since the beginning of time. No one group of people is immune to discrimination.

Somewhere in all of our pasts lie either those who were enslaved or those who enslaved others. Some even contain both instances. Unfortunately, discrimination still exists in this day and age.

Millions of people have lost their lives in the name of hatred although those who have contributed to their deaths would insist on calling it something else. Any reason you can name and you will find innocent people have been slaughtered because of it.

Let's get back to Iqaluit. As I have already mentioned, anger and resentment run deep in the Inuit people which is intensified by alcohol. Their true feelings come through and are completely honest.

On one of my midnight shifts, I was approached by an Inuit woman who wanted me to connect her to her cousin staying at the hotel. After four or five times with no answer, I finally told her she needed to leave. She began to protest, insisting she needed to speak with her cousin.

By this time, Hank, the security guard had arrived. I told the young woman – again– she needed to leave. This time I also added that if she didn't leave, I would call the cops. Again, she protested.

Hank then spoke up. "What's going on?" he asked.

The girl pointed a finger at me and said, "She won't let me talk to my cousin!" She stared at him in a drunken haze.

Hank eyed me as I calmly responded. "I already tried to connect you a few times and there was no answer." She kept insisting that I had to connect her to his room despite her not getting a response from her cousin.

When I again told her she had to leave I would call the police, she turned to Hank, in hopes he would help her out."She's the boss," he told her as I dialed them.

Hank escorted her as far as the front steps outside but she was refusing to leave. He was still out there when the Mounties arrived. When the officer asked her what was going on, Hank said the young woman pointed inside and said, "I don't like that girl inthere. She won't let me talk to my cousin."

Hank explained to the officers I had tried to connect her several times but there was no answer in the room. "And I don't like you, either," she said, looking at him.

When Hank came back in, he was laughing. When he told me what had happened, I couldn't help laughing myself. I buried my face in my hands, pretending to be hurt and offended. "I can't believe she doesn't like me," I wailed.

Both Hank and I laughed about that night for weeks after. This incident had occurred not long after a similar incident with him.

An Inuit woman – I would say she was in her late forties – was standing by the front entrance, obviously in a drunken stupor. When she dropped a few items from her hands, Hank bent over to pick them up former.

"Here ya go, ma'am," he said, handing them to her.

"You're from Newfoundland, aren't you?" she asked, no emotion in her voice.

Hank nodded. "Yes, ma'am, I am," he answered, proudly.

"I hate you. I hate you all," she stated, again no emotion in her voice whatsoever.

When Hank asked her why, she just said her son-in-law was a Newfie and she didn't like them."Twice in about a week you had someone tell you they don't like you," I observed shortly after.

He buried his face in his hands as I had. "I don't know if I can handle people not liking me," he quipped.

GIMME ALL YOU'RE MONEY!

Throughout my time living in the Arctic, I was never afraid to walk by myself at night. In Iqaluit, I would often walk to work – or from, depending upon my shift –late at night. Since I lived only a short five-minute walk from where I worked, it usually wasn't a problem anyway.

Shortly after midnight one night, I headed down my usual route to where my apartment was located. It was early December so anyone who was out and about was dressed for the winter weather in Iqaluit.

As I was saying, I was walking the direct path to where I lived when I saw a guy walking up towards the hotel. I moved to one side so the young man could pass by. Instead, he grabbed my throat and pulled out a long knife. "Gimme all your money!" he demanded.

I was startled but only for a split-second. Calmness came over me. It was almost as if someone had taken over my body. "I don't have any money," I answered.

I had ten dollars in my bag but I was not about to dig for it. I don't know what he would have done if I tried. The guy insisted again that I give him my money. "Look, I already told you that I have no money."

My eyes stared into his dark ones. Since he was wearing a ski mask, his eyes were all I could see. "And I think you're fucking stupid to do this behind the cop shop." I hadn't gotten further than just behind the RCMP detachment, which was about halfway between the hotel and where I lived. He didn't seem to be phased by this.

"I suppose you want to die?" he asked, trying to sound menacing. Obviously, he didn't know who he was talking to.

I grew up in the north end of Dartmouth, which is known as one of the toughest parts of the city. "Go right ahead," I dared, raising my eyebrow.

He then proceeded to stab at me with the knife. With how close we were to each other – he still had a hold of my throat – I should have felt the stabbing but I didn't.

After what seemed forever, the mugger seemed to have been spooked by something or someone behind me. He shoved me to the ground and took off running.

I stood and momentarily considered going home. Instead, I turned and made my way to the RCMP station. By the time I arrived, I was in tears. I don't think it had hit me until that point what might have happened but I think the adrenaline had begun to finally wear off.

The officers led me to a small room with some pens and paper. While I was writing my statement about what had happened, the Mountiesand his partner took off to see if they could find him. It seemed to be an eternity before they returned – far too much time for me to think about what had happened.

When the officer finally came back into the room, I was a nervous wreck. I then told him exactly what had occurred. I couldn't give him a description of the guy because his face was covered with a ski mask. All I knew was that he was a young Inuit male. How did I know this? What I could see of his eyes, there was no wrinkling and I knew by the way he spoke that he was native.

The officer gave me a drive home to make certain I at least made it there without another incident. You would think after this mugging, I would be prejudiced against the Inuit but I wasn't. I was angry and upset but didn't hate them.

I had realized that the majority of them were fabulous people. Just because I had been violated by a few doesn't mean I should hold the entire group responsible. I had made friends with many of them so I couldn't find it in my heart to blame them all for the actions of a few.

I hadn't realized how traumatized I was by the mugging until I tried to go to sleep that night. I would see his eyes whenever I closed mine. It was only when I put on my Terry Bradshaw jersey that I was able to calm down enough for me to get some sleep.

Terry has been an idol of mine for a long time and I had made a promise to myself that if I ever had a chance to meet him, I would give him a great big hug and thank him for saving my life. When I returned home to Nova Scotia, I had heard he was filming a movie in Halifax.

Although I never had the opportunity to see him face to face, I was able to speak with him and thank him. He insisted he didn't do anything to save my life but I know different. I still owe him a great big hug.

What about my mugger? To this day, he is still free as far as I know. I needed to increase my anti-depressant medication and go to therapy afterwards but he got away with a crime. But I grew stronger because of it because it proved to me I was a survivor.

ALL HE HAD TO DO WAS ASK

In April of 2003, I was half-way through a one-year contract as a front desk and housekeeping supervisor. Rankin Inlet was a vast contrast to my experience in Iqaluit.The Inuit there were phenomenal. Even while they were intoxicated, they were pretty laid-back. I thoroughly enjoyed my time in Rankin Inlet except for one incident.

In mid-April, we had the eye clinic come to the hotel. The eye clinic consists of an optometrist, ophthalmologist, assistant and booking clerk.

Late one afternoon, an Inuit elder came into the hotel, looking for the eye doctor. His comprehension of English seemed limited so when he didn't understand my directions, I motioned for him to follow me.I led him down the hallway to where the booking clerk was situated. I gestured towards the boardroom and then it happened. The elder copped a feel of my right breast.

I was momentarily stunned, unsure if what had just happened really happened. Byte time I returned to the front desk, it had sunk in. I tried to make light of it but I was feeling extremely violated.

When my front desk clerk, Raina, told me he had done it before but was never formally charged with it, I found that I was muchangrier than violated. I went to my office and proceeded to call the RCMP.I explained to them what had happened.

I asked them how I could prevent him from doing it to other women – especially to young women who were fourteen or fifteen who didn't know it was wrong – without charging him. I was more concerned with protecting these girls than I was about my own well-being.

The officer explained the only way I could do that was to charge him with sexual assault. If he had a criminal record, he may be dissuaded from re-offending. Or if he did re-offend, he would face stiffer sentences for every subsequent violation. So I agreed to pursue charges and booked an appointment for the following afternoon.

After I filled out the paperwork, Officer Parker asked me how I found out the man's name. I told him Riana, the front desk clerk on duty the previous afternoon, had given me the information. He continued to advise me the man in question already had a reputation for inappropriately touchingwomen.

He agreed with me when I said there isa difference between crude remarks andogling (which I am used to have happeningto me but it never bothered me) andsomeone putting their hands on any part ofmy body without my permission. He brokethe law when he fondled my breast withoutmy consent.

I had joked afterward that if he wantedto feel my boob, all he had to do was ask. Itwas my way of trying to deal with the situation. It didn't work as I went through all of the after-effects of being sexually assaulted – feeling his hands on me, wanting to shower constantly, crying and nightmares.

My mother said I should have punchedhim out and I would have felt better. Maybeso but I probably would have been the onecharged with assault. Officer Parker told methat he and his partner would inform thesuspect of the charges pending against him.

I received a phone call from theofficer at my second job later on thatafternoon. He stated they spoke with theelder in regards to the situation at hand.The man told the officers he was sorryhe put his hands on me and he wanted to sitdown with me as well as the officers so hecould apologize. He also promised hewouldn't do it again.

I wanted to laugh. Was this guyserious? "He may not do it to ME again," I responded. "But that's not going to stophim from doing to someone else who didn'tknow it was wrong." Officer Parker thenasked me if I wanted to go forward with thecase.

When I said yes, he responded, "Good girl. I told him he picked the wrong woman this time." I had to smile. It felt good doingthe right thing.

This pervert needed to know hecouldn't just touch a woman's private partsand think he could get away with it. Justapologizing for it will not make the problemgo away. This man needed to pay forbreaking the law and if I had to be the firstto go through with it completely, then so beit. I was proud of myself for standing upand doing the right thing.

Those around me though had other ideas. I was asked if really wanted to open that can of worms. I was asked why I was charging him because he only touched my breast.I couldn't believe what I was hearing. How could these women really ask me such questions? Do they not realize that a crime had been committed? A crime committed against one of their sisters?

I thought, 'What if he did it to them? Would they think or feel any different?' Did they not understand he had gotten away with this before because his accusers were convinced to drop the charges? In the meantime, his victims were dealing with the aftereffects of being violated. They and I all felt dirty, violated and devalued. It took me a long time to overcome the feelings of being personally defiled.

The morning after this man touched me, I took the short walk down to where the optometrist and booking clerk were situated. I had realized after I went home the night before that I had left this man alone with the young woman. I asked her if he had tried anything with her and if she was okay.

She said he had made some suggestive comments but she had managed to keep him away from her until Phil had returned. She also reassured me she was alright. I felt so relieved. I would have felt even guiltier if anything had happened to her because I had abandoned her with this louse.

Of all who knew of what happened, Phil, the optometrist and Raina, the front desk clerk were the only two people who backed me up in regards to thecrime. That is, other than the RCMP, of course, because they knew of his history and wanted to prevent him from doing it again. I think they were thankful someone finally came forward who had the courage not to back down because of outside pressure.

Although I was upset when he received six months' probation, I was alsohappy he finally had a criminal record. It meant any future charges against him would result in stiffer sentences.

IF ONLY I HAD BEEN WITH HER

One woman I had befriended while I was in Rankin Inlet was Anna, one of the housekeeping staff at the hotel. Anna was a very tiny woman. She was less than five feet tall and I doubt she weighed a hundred pounds soaking wet.

I don't usually take notice of another person's height unless they are shorter than I am. I am so used to being around people who are considerable taller than I am that when I come in contact with someone who's shorter than I am, I immediately pay attention.

Anna was one of the sweetest people I had ever come in contact with. I thoroughly enjoyed spending time with her even through most of the time it was over coffee.

Anna, like the rest of the housekeeping staff, was phenomenal in her job. But unlike the others, she wanted to do something other than clean rooms. Anna desperately wanted to work in the dining room. In my opinion, she would have done very well in the dining room.

She enjoyed serving others and she did everything in her power to make people happy. She was always in high spirits and verysociable. Just before New Year's, Anna had asked me to her place for a few drinks. I already had plans for that evening so impolitely declined. For about a month prior to this, Anna had become rather fond of a man she had been working for on a part-time basis.

He was married but his wife was living in Winnipeg. As much as I tried to convince her she could do better than a married man, Anna was far too enamored to listen to anything but her heart.

I can't fault the woman for I believe you can't control who you fall in love with. For women like Anna and me, it usually doesn't take much for us to become smitten with someone. A kind word is sometimes all it takes because we hear them so seldom and our self-esteem is so low, we believe the person giving us the compliment cares about us.

I've been in a similar position as Anna. We crave as much attention as we can muster but unfortunately, much of the attention we receive is detrimental to our mental and emotional well-being.To this day, I still bear the scars of choosing the wrong men but I am stronger now because of that and I am much more content with whom I am. I realize I do not need a man to define me as a person.

But back to Anna. The night she had asked me to her place for drinks and a few games of cards, I had declined her invitation but had promised her I would do so on another night. The next morning, I come to work expecting to see Anna later and asking her how her night went. The looks on the faces of management, I knew something was wrong.

It was then that Angela, the general manager, told me Anna was found in a pile of snow with nothing but a nightgown on. The man she was seeing lived nearby and inhere drunken state of mind, she was walkingto see him.

To say I was a wreck would be an understatement. I felt so guilty. If I had only changed my plans and gone to her gathering, Anna would still be alive.

Those around me had tried to console me, telling me she would have gone even if I had been there. I wouldn't have been able to stop her. There would have been no way I could have been with her the entire night. If she was determined to go, she was going regardless of what time it was.

I had to agree with that analysis but it still didn't make me feel any better. To die of hypothermia is a tragic way to go.

The male staff of the hotel served as her pallbearers and to know this beautiful woman would no longer be a part of our lives hurt us all very deeply. Telling stories about her in the days after helped many of us to cope with her death.

WHERE ARE YOUR EYES?

One of the most rewarding jobs I had while I was working in the north was at the group home which provided shelter to children with disabilities. I absolutely adored each and every one of them. They always made me laugh, sometimes so hard I ended up with tears running down my face.

Many times, they would tell stories about their day around the supper table. The youngest one, Jerry, who was five, would often mimic what the older children were saying as most youngsters are apt to do.

The male manager at the time looked directly into the boy's eyes and lectured, "Now, Jerry, we discussed this before. You know the difference between fact and fiction."

All I could do was sit and stare at this man. I couldn't believe I was hearing him correctly. My only thought – which was screaming in my head – was, 'He's five!He doesn't know the words fact and fiction. He's five! He just wants to be like the other kids. He knows he's just making up stories. We ALL know he's just making it up but he's five!'

Every five-year-old I ever knew and I knew a lot because my mother babysat often, enjoyed using their imagination. Everyone at the table knew Jerry was only making it up but there was no need to scold the child in front of the other children, if atoll. I wish to this day I had said something but I cannot change the past.

Usually if I was working the evening shift at the group home, I would bring in movies for the kids to watch. As with any other child, they liked movies with other kids and movies with animals.

One evening, I was getting everything set up when I spied two of the children picking on Luke. I saw their reflections on the television set but they didn't know this.Without turning around, I said, "Both of you knock it off right now." I didn't raise my voice but they knew by my tone that I wasn't joking around.

"How did you know what we were doing?" asked Peter.

"I have eyes in the back of my head," I answered as I turned on the set and began the movie. I took a seat next to Luke on the sofa and he started digging around my hair. "Luke, what are you doing?"

"I trying to find your eyes. Where are they?" he asked. "I want to see them." This was one of those times I was laughing so hard the tears were running down my face. I had forgotten that sometimes these kids took everything we said literally.

"They're invisible, Luke. You can't see them." My answer seemed to satisfy his curiosity and he turned around to concentrate on the movie.

The kids I looked after at the group home amazed me almost on a daily basis. As with any other child, they had their strengths and weakness as well as their likes and dislikes.

Luke loved science and technology. For his birthday the year before, he was given a book on the solar system. I think he had it memorized but he still went through it with great gusto.

One day, I was opening a bag of cookies and Luke was standing nearby, watching me. He then started to motion how the automated assembly line worked.

"How did you know that, Luke?" I asked him. He just shrugged his shoulders. I think he saw it on television at some point and he remembered it.

Sarah, one of the two girls at the group home, loved music and her favorite singer was Susan Aglukark. One night, I brought in my Cyndi Lauper greatest hits CD just for a change of pace. Sarah seemed to enjoy the music so I thought I would bring it in again when I had my one-on-one time with her.

A few days later, she was in the tub and singing each song from the CD in order. She didn't have all the words memorized but she knew the majority. That answered my question of whether she really liked Cyndi Lauper. At that very moment, I remembered she had a birthday coming up in about a month so I thought I would order her the compact disc.

It arrived on her birthday and when she opened it, I thought she was going to go through the ceiling, she was so excited. Just seeing the joy on her face was thanks enough for me but I gladly took the great big hug from her as well.

One of the other boys, Andy, loved anything that had to do with construction. He could tell you the difference between many vehicles that were on construction site.

He was also very good at the card game, Concentration. I don't think I ever won a game against him. I don't remember the strengths of the other children as the turnover was high and I didn't have much of a chance to know them.

WOULDN'T IT BE FUNNY IF-?

As I mentioned in my prologue, my time in the Arctic had both positive and negative experiences. I contend each event I witnessed or endured has made me stronger person.

It is my belief our character is built by everyone we meet and by everything we go through. It has been more than tenyears since my last trip to the Arctic and looking back upon my tenure, I would have to say my positive experiences far outnumber the negative.

Part of me misses being in the north but I think my time of living and working in the Arctic has run its course. I'm not discounting the possibility of visiting the north since I have yet to go to the Yukon.

I just don't think I have it in me to reside there anymore. It's time for me to cut my ties with my love affair with the frozen tundra although it will always have a special place in my heart.

But there is one incident that will probably haunt me for the rest of my life. You would think it would be the death of my good friend, Anna, but you would be mistaken.

It would be an incident that happened about four years earlier. I was living in Iqaluit, working at the hotel as a front desk agent. The hotel provided us with housing that we shared with other employees of the hotel.

Two of the kitchen staff, Mike and Charles, lived together in one of the company apartments. Mike was from Nova Scotia and Charles was an Inuit who I think was from Pond Inlet.

Charles was a talented artist and would work on his sculptures when he wasn't at his job in the kitchen. Mike was a cook's helper and I think his only extracurricular activity was drinking.

Before he moved in with Charles, there was a rumor around town that Mike had poisoned a previous roommate when he worked at a different establishment. But it was simply a rumor since there was no conclusive evidence to state otherwise.

Outward appearances had Mike and Charles seemingly getting along like the best of friends. The two men spent a lot of their free time together and it was usually spent at the bar.

About a month later, Charles failed to show up for one of his shifts. Phone calls went unanswered as did visits to his apartment. Their other roommate, Jeff, stated he hadn't seen Charles in nearly a week.

On the third day of Charles 'mysterious absence, Mike and Jeff returned home from work together. Before they headed upstairs, Mike turned to Jeff and said, "Wouldn't it be funny if we found Charles hanging in his closet?"

Jeff found this statement odd and considering the fact that Charles was quite tall, for him to hang himself in a closet that would make it nearly impossible for anybody to kill themselves in such manner, didn't make any sense to him or to anyone else. Jeff doubted he would find Charles in the closet but he went in anyway.

When he opened the sliding door and saw his roommate with a rope around his neck, Jeff immediately felt sick. His first thought returned to Mike. It seemed peculiar to him that the one statement he uttered out of the blue had come to fruition. While the case was considered a suicide, many of us were skeptical considering the circumstantial evidence.

MIDGE

One of the best people I ever met while I was living in Iqaluit was Joe, one of the property managers. A day never went by when he didn't come into the hotel and make me laugh.

We had a daily ritual of an arm-wrestling contest which he always won. I actually looked forward to the daily challenge. It was usually the only bright spot in my day on my second venture to working at the hotel.

While I was off for a few months, a new general manager had taken over and his head was filled with misinformation in regards to me from different staff members. Unfortunately, the front desk manager was off on maternity leave so she couldn't give him the true story. Unlike other staff, I never complained about any shift I was given and I never whined about any extra work I was offered.

In fact, I rather enjoyed doing different tasks. It kept me from becoming bored. Holly, the front desk manager, often would have me do her collection calls because she thought I sounded more aggressive than she did.

But when I returned after my two months, it was far too late. The general manager had already made his mind up about me and my work habits. Unfortunately, none of it was good.

Joe was my bright spot. When he found out one day that the general manager had accused me of discussing hotel business with him, he was fuming. Joe stormed into the general manager's office and tore a strip off him.

How dare he accuse either one of us of discussing confidential information! The general manager informed him that Joe was spending a lot of time at the front desk while was working so what else could we be discussing but hotel business. Joe was getting angrier by the second.

He considered me to be a friend and the only thing we talked about was the goings on in our life and the happenings around town. He said to the general manager that I was far too professional total about what was going on with the hotel.

When Joe found out – not from me but one of the hotel patrons who were at the front desk at the time – that the general manager berated me in front of him and accusing me of complaining to Joe about my previous scolding, he was fuming again. Into the office he went again to give the man a piece of his mind.

I couldn't have asked for a better friend than Joe. If it wasn't for him, I don't know how I could have stood living in Iqaluit.

He even provided me with a nickname use to this day and I would have to say it is one of my favorites. He had come in one day for his morning coffee and greeted me with, "Hey, Midge, how are things?"

"Midge?" I asked.

"Yeah, Midge. Its short for midget and you're short," he answered, laughing.

How could I argue with that logic? Midge is a shortened version of midget and at five feet tall, I am short. I absolutely love the nickname and whenever I think about it, I still laugh out loud even though it has been more than ten years.

TRACILYN, IS IT FUNNY?

I know there is a saying that you're not supposed to have a favorite among children but I couldn't stop it from happening. Luke was by far my favorite of the children at the group home although I never showed favoritism while I was working. But Luke was constantly surprising me with what he knew but more than that, he always made me laugh without knowing he was.

One Sunday afternoon, I decided I wanted to take all the children out to see movie. I had taken them out before but usually I take them out to the restaurant for dinner. I was constantly surprised by how well behaved they were and how well they used their manners.

I always allowed them to make their own orders which they always did with a please and a thank you. One night, I had taken them when two consultants from "Sesame Park" were at the hotel.

I was amazed that one of them – a big man about six foot five inches and 300 pounds – kneeled down so he could talk to the kids eye to eye. Of course, the kids were pestering to know where Elmo was until I finally had to tell them he was upstairs in bed asleep.

For dessert, I treated them all to one of my favorites - chocolate mousse since they missed out meeting their favorite Muppet. That's when Luke piped up and asked, "Me eat moose? Me eat Bullwinkle?" Trying not laugh, I explained to him it wasn't that kind of moose but from then on, it was his favorite dessert when they went out to the hotel for meals.

But let's get back to the movie. One of the other caregivers went with us as an extra set of eyes and hands. I never had issues with handling the children alone before but the managers didn't seem to like me much since the children had a tendency to listen to me more than to them. There were other issues too but it all went back tothem and their way of managing.

In the theatre, I was seated between Luke and Jerry. The kids like the Muppets and the movie we took them to see was "Muppets from Space." They laughed throughout the movie but at one point early in the show; Luke tapped me on the arm and asked, "Tracilyn, is it funny?"

I turned to him and asked, "Luke, did you laugh?"

He chuckled and said, "Yes, it is funny." I think he just wanted to make sure it was okay for him to enjoy the movie.

HALBERT

My first general manager in the north was Hal. I didn't actually meet him until two weeks after I arrived in Iqaluit. He was on vacation in Cuba at the time.

Hal and I hit it off immediately. He appreciated my sense of humor and when problems arose, he listened to both sides of the issue before he made a decision.

One instance was when the night auditor, Tiny, complained to Hal about me and my apparent attitude. He told Hal I was moody and took things out on my fellow coworkers because apparently I was promised supervisory position.

When I came in for my three pm shift, Hal took me aside and asked me what I was promised when I was hired. Not knowing the situation, I was confused. "Well," I answered. "You promised me my flight up, housing, meals and $10 an hour after my probation period."

"Did I ever promise you a supervisory position?"

I shook my head. "No. Only what I already mentioned. Why?"

Hal laughed his big jolly laugh. "Because Tiny's been saying otherwise. He said you've been moody and taking things out on the rest of the staff."

I giggled. "Really? Me? Moody? Maybe it's him and he's just projecting his feelings on me."

Hal agreed. "Don't worry about it. Kinda figured as much but I just wanted to hear what you had to say about the situation. Don't say anything to him tonight when he comes in to relieve you. I'll deal with him in the morning."

Tiny would forever have a hate on for me but I'm sure I wasn't the only one he despised. He was part of the plot against me a year or so later when I returned to Iqaluit the second time. I think he was jealous of me because I gave off a confident vibe.

I began calling my general manager Halbert early on in my contract. He found it amusing and he never told me not to call him that. He knew I meant it in a good way and it wasn't done in jest. At the time, I was into the 'Dilbert' comic strip so the transition was easy for me.

One afternoon, I was leaving for the day and Tara was relieving me. Hal considered himself quite the ladies' man but Tara and I didn't see it. We drew caricature of him with sweat coming down his arms with lines of odor surround him.

I drew a rat lying on his back with all four paws in the air. In a speech bubble above the rat and then I wrote, "Why is everything getting so dark? I'm dying ….dying..."

I ran it upstairs, shoved it under his door and took off back downstairs. By the time I reached the front desk, he was already on the phone with Tara. She handed it to me and I heard him say, "You know the two of you are crazy but I love it. I'm going to keep this picture to remind me of you two nuts."

HOW WAS I SUPPOSED TO KNOW?

I had mentioned in one of my previous stories about the new general manager of the hotel had been influenced by different members of the male staff. He had preconceived ideas of me before I even returned to work. The odds were against me ever being happy working the front desk anymore.

Holly, the front desk manager, once said I was constantly smiling coming in for my shifts before the change of management. Now, I dreaded coming in because I didn't know what type of trouble I would be in the moment I walked through the front door.

Before the new general manager, I was always cracking jokes with the other staff and with the guests. In fact, we would constantly have guests hanging out at the front desk because we were always happy and having fun.

The regulars looked forward to when Tara and I would do our shift changes. The two of us were always poking fun at each other. Sometimes the guests would get involved with our ongoing gags and this only made them want to spend more time around us.

I had asked one of them one time why they liked spending so much time around us. He said we were the only department who seemingly got along and enjoyed being around each other.

But Tom, the new general manager, didn't seem to appreciate the camaraderie. I began working for the government during the day just to get away from the constant criticism. It had gotten to the point that no one was happy working at the hotel.

One evening, I had gotten a phone call from a concerned man from Nova Scotia. It was a slow night so I had no problem answering any questions he had when it came to Iqaluit. He said his eighteen-year-olddaughter was thinking about coming up to work at the hotel and he wanted to make sure it was good idea. I answered his questions as honestly as I could.

When he asked me if I had an eighteen-year-old child, would I want her up there? I said I wouldn't want her here. Eighteen was a bit young to endure the cruel reality of what went on in Iqaluit. He thanked me and hung up.

The next morning – a Saturday – Tom called me at home, fuming. "How dare you tell someone not to come up and work at the hotel," he yelled. When I tried to explain what had happened, he just called me a liar, that I was always lying and I was fired.

Thankfully, I had my government job but I now needed to find an apartment. My buddy, Joe, helped me out and found me an apartment in one of the complexes he managed. I don't know what I would have done if it wasn't for him.

When I stopped into the hotel to buy paper and say hi to one of the front desk clerks, the bartender on early duty started chew me out in front of the entire lobby. Instead of responding, I just took my paper, turned around and went back to my apartment.

How was I supposed to know the man I was speaking with was the father of one of the new staff members recently hired? The man only told me his daughter was considering coming to Iqaluit, not that she had been offered a job.

Holly had emailed me and told me to worry about it. They were just mad because I spoke the truth. At least I had someone on my side.

MOMENTARY MELTDOWN

I think that with almost every trip I took to the north, I was tested with a tragic event that would have me examining my resolve. One such event hit very close to home. I usually called home at least once awake to catch up on any news.

At the end of August 1999, I phoned home and was speaking with my mother. She asked me if I remembered Carolyn and AllanMcCullough. Of course, I did. Al and Carolyn were good friends with my late father. Dad and Carolyn did a lot of charity work together.

It was then she dropped a bombshell. Theirnineteen-year-old son, Jason, was brutally murdered a few nights earlier. He was walking home through a park around the corner from where I lived in Dartmouth. He had been shot at point-blank range in the back of his head.

To this day, over ten years later, the case is still unsolved. The news was shocking but I thought I had it under control. Shortly after I hung up, I prepared for work and then made my way to the hotel for my three pm shift. I guess I wasn't acting myself because Holly, the front desk manager, asked me if I was alright.

I shook my head. "The son of a family friend was murdered a few nights ago. They don't know whodid it or why he was killed." At that moment, I think reality finally sunk in and I had acomplete meltdown. I became a blithering idiot and couldn't stop crying.

I made it through about an hour of my shift. Holly then stepped in after I had tried to ask Tara to relieve me. She took the phone to see if she was able to take over the shift. When she came in, she asked what Tom did this time.I had to tell her, through waves of sobbing, that it had nothing to do with our new general manager. I think it took me twenty minutes to explain what was going on.

I then took the short walk home. My roommate, Gina, who was also Tara's cousin, made certain that I didn't do anything drastic. They all knew of my history of bulimia. They understood, from what I told them, throwing up was my way of dealing with stressful situations and coping with uncomfortable circumstances.

Although I hadn't made myself vomit in years, the death of a young man –especially in the manner in which he died –who had his whole life in front of him had me in a such a state that I would have gone back to my coping mechanism.

Fortunately, I made it through this traumatic experience without my lifelong companion of bulimia. I have to thank thoseI had surrounded myself with for getting me through the rough patch.

WHAT HAPPENED TO SUNDAY?

My experience with drunks in Iqaluit for the most part has been anything but pleasant. Their true identities would emerge after a night of drinking. They were often mean, surly and down-right ignorant. Whatever came into their heads would immediately be uttered without worry of the consequence.

They didn't care about anything except venting their anger and frustration and it didn'tmatter where they directed it. As long as they were fulfilling their needs, it didn't matter who they hurt in the process. I have to say I know sober people who do the something and many of those people are sociopaths.

At least those who are drunk or high have an excuse for why they act the way they do. I don't know how many times I was accused of taking jobs away from the Inuit or have them call me by some type of slur.

As much as I understand their hatred and their rage towards white people, it still hurt very deeply. I never did anything tothem but yet I was being blamed for everything that had happened to them in theirnot so distant past. It was a rarity in Iqaluit to encounter an intoxicated Inuit who was pleasant.

So when an Inuit woman in her mid-forties came in on Sunday morning and was very sweet, it took those of us working on the desk by surprise to learn she was intoxicated. She wanted to go upstairs to visit her brother but the hotel had a policy of not allowing people who were under the influence to go to the rooms where the guests were staying.

The woman seemed to take it all in stride especially when she was allowed to call up to the room. When she found out her cousin wasn't in the room, she was satisfied. Instead of leaving, she decided she would visit with us. I was standing off to the side, eating my supper while my counterpart, Tara, was working the desk.

The woman asked her what day it was. "It's Sunday," Tara answered.

The woman looked at her, confused. What happened to Sunday?" she asked.

Again, Tara told her it was Sunday. "But I was drinking on Saturday," she went on. "And I was drinking today but I don't know what happened to Sunday."

By this time, Tara and I were laughing so hard, we were crying. Even the woman was laughing although she had no idea we were laughing because of her.

The following night, I was having dinner with my friend, Mary at the Qamatik Inn and I told her what had happened. "I think she was your mother," I added. Mary looked exactly like our lady with the missing day.

"My mother doesn't drink," Mary told me. "It sounds like she may have been my aunt." I still wonder to this day if she ever figured out where Sunday disappeared to.

YOUR TEAM IS GOING DOWN TOMORROW!

About a month and a half after my mugging, I was looking forward to watching the Super Bowl. My team, the Pittsburgh Steelers, was playing against the Seattle Seahawks. Because I was dealing with posttraumatic stress, anything to take my mind off what had happened – even if only for a few hours – would be welcome.

I rarely asked for a Sunday off so when I asked for Super Bowl Sunday, the front desk manager obliged. The Storehouse Bar was given permission to open as well for the big game. So my plan for Super Bowl Sunday was beginning to take shape.Being able to watch my boys on the big screen as they played in Detroit while having a few drinks was just what the doctor ordered. I needed one day to not worry about the trauma I was going through.

The day before Super Bowl XL, I was working four to midnight on the front desk. I was going through my game plan in my head for the following day when five guys had arrived to check in.One of them was wearing a Seattle Seahawks hat. Before they could say anything, I laughed and said, "Your team is going down tomorrow."

They immediately perked up and one of the older men said, "What? No welcome to the Frobisher Inn?"

"So sorry, welcome to the Frobisher Inn and by the way, your team is going down tomorrow." We were still joking around while I checked them into the hotel. Once, I handed them their key cards, I let them know the hotel bar was going to be open for the game. "Hope you can make it, "I told them. "It's going to be a good game."

The next afternoon, I prepared myself for watching my team playing. I put on my Terry Bradshaw jersey with black pants, socks and boots. I French braided my hair into two braids which were secured with my Pittsburgh Steelers scrunches. After my trip to the bank, I made my way to the Storehouse.

Since the bar wasn't open yet, I hung out at the front desk with Hank and Ellie. "I don't think I've ever seen you in such good mood in a long time," Ellie observed.

"You could say I'm excited," I answered. "This is my Christmas."

When the Storehouse finally opened, I headed down the hallway and found myself table close to the big screen. I ordered some appetizers along with a Captain dark and Coke. Shortly after, I saw my Seattle buddies come in and sit at a long table nearby.

I signaled to my server after the guys were halfway through their first round of drinks. I told her I would like to buy their next round. Just because they were cheering for the wrong team, it didn't mean I couldn't be a good sport. When they received their drinks, they lifted their glasses as a gesture of thanks.

About five minutes before the game started, one of them came over and invited me to join them. "We can't have you sitting alone," he said. gladly accepted their invitation. I don't remember having such a good time in long time. At least in recent memory since until that point, I was going through a rough patch in my life.

I love football. It is by far my favorite sport although hockey is a very close second. Unlike the Stanley Cup though, the Super Bowl is one game – winner take all. Teams in the hockey playoffs have several games to win each level. Partway through the game, I was tapped on the shoulder by one of the patrons. "This isn't the Stanley Cup, you know," he informed me.

I grinned. "No. It's better. It's the Super Bowl!"

By the end of the game, I was thoroughly intoxicated but ecstatic. My Steelers had eked out a win and my prophecy from the previous day had come to fruition. I came out of the bar with my fists pumping in the air. "Whoo-hoo!" I exclaimed which made Ellie and Hank laugh. "I'm drunk and I don't care," I continued.

When I took over for Ellie the next afternoon, I apologized for my behavior the previous night. She just laughed. "Don't worry about that. It was good to see you smiling and happy. We haven't seen you like that in a long time."

It was good for me. I needed one day where I could enjoy myself and not worry about the world around me.

FORTY LASHINGS WITH A WET NOODLE

On one of Hal's trips to Cuba, he had left the Executive Chef in charge of running the hotel. Brad, like Tiny, didn't much like me although he never openly admitted it or showed his disdain.

It seemed odd I was attracting such scorn but at the time I didn't have the 20-20 vision I now possess. I now believe these men were intimidated by me.

Although, as one co-worker said, I was a Pillsbury doughboy, I put forth an air of confidence and toughness. Deep down, I was an insecure young woman, incapable of trusting anyone. I think I acted tougher on the outside to cover up the frightened little girl I was on the inside.

It took a long time for my inside to catch up to what I was showing on the outside. I think it almost flip-flopped. I'm now crusty on the inside and my outer shell appears to be softer.

Then again, maybe I'm a good blend of both but I reiterate, it took me a long time to build up my inner self-assurance. Back then, I guess the males I worked with didn't know any different.

Apparently, I didn't know my own strength and character.

One day, Brad had left the hotel for the day but had forgotten to close and lock the doors to Hal's office. Hal had amassed great deal of art from the locals and he kept them in his office. I had come up for my meal and when I was finished eating, I noticed both doors were wide open. I asked Tara if Brad was still around. She said no, that he had gone home for the day.

A sudden though hit me and I started to giggle. I went into Hal's office and took out a written warning sheet from the file cabinet. "What are you doing?" Tara asked.

"Brad left the doors to Hal's office open. I think he would be upset if any of his art went missing so I think Brad should be written up," I answered, chuckling even more. In the punishment section, I wrote that the employee in question should receive forty lashings with a wet noodle. I don't think Tara and I stopped laughing the entire time.

Actually, Tara and I did a lot of laughing when we were together and we were always up to no good. Tara was usually the instigator and I was the grunt who put the plans into action. This time it was different. This time, it was all me.

I put the warning letter on the desk for Brad to find it the next morning. I then closed both doors and made sure they were locked. Brad pretended he found the whole thing humorous but we all knew better. He told me he had thrown the letter in the garbage.

When Hal came back, I told him about the whole incident. When he finally stopped laughing, he asked me if I had a copy of the warning, I said no and he told me that he wished I had made a photocopy of it just so he could see it for himself.

SECURITY!

One night, I was working the night audit shift. I rather enjoyed the back shift. After the bar let out, it was quiet and you were rarely disturbed.

I found the shift rather relaxing once we were ride of all of the drunks out of the hallway. Fortunately, the property management company had hired security guards to patrol the mall area and other properties in town.

One security guard was Ted, a hunk oaf man that many of us girls drooled over. He was on duty the same night I was doing the audit shift and I felt immediately safer.

After I finished the audit, I began to prepare for the next few hours of peace and quiet. I no sooner sat down to read and listen to music than the phone rang. It was Michel, the head chef who had taken over for Brad. He was in a panic and wanted meto call the police.

"Why?" I asked. "What's going on and why can't you call them? I'll give you the number."

"No. I want you to call them. It sounds like someone is getting strangled next door," he insisted. I didn't understand why he wanted me to call the cops. I had no information to give them except for the apartment number.

Instead of the police, I called Ted and told him what little information I did know. It was procedure that we call security before calling the RCMP. Ted went down to the White Row unit in question along with the police.

They heard what Michel was hearing – a woman screaming in agony. When they didn't receive an answer to the doorbell, the police broke open the door and rushed inside. What they found was bunch of teenagers having a Scope party.

What about the screaming woman? It was a CD the kids were listening to while they were drinking the mouthwash. When he returned to the hotel and told me what had happened, all I could do was shake my head.

Ted had to get some extra information from me so he could fill out his report of the incident. Neither one of us could understand why Michel refused to call security himself.

"How are you supposed to give proper information if you don't know the whole situation? I mean, seriously, you are here so you can't really tell us anything down there."

I shrugged. "I don't know what to tell ya. Maybe he isn't used to doing anything for himself."

To this day, I still don't know what was going through the man's head but at least, there was nothing extremely serious going on next door to him.

EPILOGUE

While writing these stories, I have learned a lot about myself. They gave me the opportunity to take a serious look at who I am now as compared to when I made my initial trip to the Great White North.

Although I put forth the appearance of being a person of confidence, inside I am anervous wreck and extremely insecure. But with each trip, I encountered some adversity that would strengthen my inner self. I realize now my entire being is more in balance. When I first started to look back upon my experiences in the north, I only remembered the worst of times.

I could have written more but these are the most significant to me. Now that I've completed my short stories, I also realize I had the best of times as well. Sometimes, the best came as result of the worst. I am now able to look at all my experience and glean only the positive from them.

My soul may have been battered and bruised in the process but I survived. It is my sincere belief I survived for a reason. God has a plan for me and I contend we all go through the best and worst scenarios throughout our lives. It is how we live our lives beyond the worst that will define our characters.

We can either hold on to the anger and resentment for the rest of our lives or we can momentarily grieve but then let it go. We can remember the pain but we don't have to let us consume us and make us miserable.

We need to keep pushing forward - living, surviving and learning. I am now in good place in my life and I will continue to grow.

www.ingramcontent.com/pod-product-compliance
Lightning Source LLC
LaVergne TN
LVHW012126070526
838202LV00056B/5888